First World War
and Army of Occupation
War Diary
France, Belgium and Germany

15 DIVISION
Divisional Troops
Divisional Cyclist Company
3 August 1915 - 29 May 1916

WO95/1923/2

The Naval & Military Press Ltd
www.nmarchive.com
Published in association with The National Archives

Published by

The Naval & Military Press Ltd

Unit 10 Ridgewood Industrial Park,

Uckfield, East Sussex,

TN22 5QE England

Tel: +44 (0) 1825 749494

www.naval-military-press.com

www.nmarchive.com

This diary has been reprinted in facsimile from the original. Any imperfections are inevitably reproduced and the quality may fall short of modern type and cartographic standards.

© Crown Copyright
Images reproduced by permission of The National Archives, London, England, 2015.

Contents

Document type	Place/Title	Date From	Date To
Heading	WO95/1923/2		
Heading	15th Division. 15th Divl Cyclist Coy. Aug 1915-May 1916		
Miscellaneous	To Officer i/c Army Cyclist Corps Records Hounslow.	04/11/1915	04/11/1915
Miscellaneous	15 Co. Founded 23 Dec. 14	23/12/1914	23/12/1914
Heading	15th Division. 15th Divl. Cycl. Coy. Vol II For 3.8.15		
War Diary	Drouvin	03/08/1915	03/08/1915
Heading	15th Division 15th Divl. Cyclist Coy Vol III Sept. 15		
War Diary	Vaudricourt	02/09/1915	02/09/1915
War Diary	Mazingarbe	24/09/1915	25/09/1915
Heading	15th Division 15th Divl. Cyclist Coy. Vol 4 Oct 15		
War Diary	Mazingarbe	27/09/1915	27/09/1915
War Diary	Deouvin	28/09/1915	28/09/1915
War Diary	Labussiere	29/09/1915	03/10/1915
War Diary	Lapugnoy	03/10/1915	03/10/1915
War Diary	Aouchin	15/10/1915	27/10/1915
War Diary	Trenches	28/10/1915	01/11/1915
War Diary	Aouchin	02/11/1915	02/11/1915
Heading	15th Divl. Cycl. Coy. Vol. 5. November 1915		
War Diary	Aouchin	02/11/1915	13/11/1915
War Diary	Drouvin	14/11/1915	30/11/1915
Heading	15th Divl. Cycl. Coys. Vol 6 December 1915		
War Diary	Drouvin	01/12/1915	15/12/1915
War Diary	Aurion Ville	16/12/1915	21/12/1915
War Diary	Minx	22/12/1915	23/12/1915
War Diary	Hurion Ville	24/12/1915	31/12/1915
Heading	15th Divl. Cyclist Vol 7		
War Diary	Hurion Ville	01/01/1916	15/01/1916
War Diary	Mazingarbe	16/01/1916	31/01/1916
Heading	15th Cyclists Vol 8		
War Diary	Mazingarbe	01/02/1916	07/02/1916
War Diary	Drouvin	08/02/1916	29/02/1916
Heading	15 Div Cycle Coy Vol 9		
War Diary	Drouvin	01/03/1916	11/03/1916
War Diary	Vaudricourt	12/03/1916	27/03/1916
War Diary	Hurion Ville	28/03/1916	01/04/1916
War Diary	Merouagne	02/04/1916	02/04/1916
War Diary	Condette	03/04/1916	17/04/1916
War Diary	Coyecques	18/04/1916	18/04/1916
War Diary	Hurion Ville	19/04/1916	26/04/1916
War Diary	Souquerial	27/04/1916	29/04/1916
Miscellaneous	To. A.G's Office Base.	29/05/1916	29/05/1916
War Diary	Fouqurreiel	01/05/1916	29/05/1916

MoMA / 1923 (c)

15TH DIVISION

15TH DIVL CYCLIST COY.

AUG 1915 - MAY 1916

To   Officer i/c Army Cyclist Corps Records
            Hounslow.

Reference your E/20139 of 29th Oct. 15 —

(I) The Company was formed on 23rd December 1914.

(II) It was recruited by volunteers from every Battalion in the 15th Division.
These men were given to understand that they would be attached to the Divisional Cyclist Company & the question of transfer to A.C.C. which came into force afterwards was not popular & some men who refused to sign their AFB 241 had to be returned to their former units.
In like manner Officers were at first seconded from their Battalions to Divisional Cyclist Companies and afterwards without any reference to the Officers concerned were transferred to A.C.C.

(III) Stations

    Woolmer Hill, Bramshot   23rd Dec 1914
                    to   27th Feb 1915
    Stockbridge, Hants   27th Feb 1915
                    to   2nd May 1915
    Chisledon Camp, Swindon   2nd May 1915
                    to   8th July 1915

8th July entrained for Southampton & reached Havre 9th July.

(IV) In LOOS on morning of 25th September 1915 Headquarters and two Platoons.
In trenches near "The Quarries" 27th October to 1st November.

(V) 2nd Lieut R.N. Chubb
2nd Lieut T.M. Duncan
No 1585 Sgt F. Scott
Recommended for mention for good work
in the field, LOOS 25th September 1915.

(VI) Drafts amounting to 22 NCO's & men
have been received.

(VII) The Company has been employed in
very numerous ways. It has furnished
many control posts. Established stores
of bombs in the trenches. Assisted Signal
Company in laying wires. Repaired roads.
Assisted A.P.M. and has acted as an
Infantry Company in the trenches.

CAPTN.,
COMMANDING 15th DIV. CYCLIST COMPY.

B.E.F
4.10.15

15 Co.

Formed 23 Dec. 14

Stationed Woolmer
              Stockbridge
              Chiseldon Camp
Left Southampton 8 July
Arrived France 9 "
Employed various duties at Loos
L in trenches near the Quarries 27 Oct to 1 Nov.
2"/Lt. R. W. Chubb }
  "   T. M. Duncan } recommended for mention
No 1585 Cpl F Scott }

15th Divnl. Cyclist Coy.

August 1915

15th Divl: Cycl: Coy:
vol: II
3. 8. 15

Army Form C. 2118.

WAR DIARY
or
~~INTELLIGENCE SUMMARY~~
(Erase heading not required.)

Instructions regarding War Diaries and Intelligence Summaries are contained in F. S. Regs., Part II. and the Staff Manual respectively. Title pages will be prepared in manuscript.

[Stamp: 15th DIVISIONAL CYCLIST COMPANY * ORDERLY ROOM * No. 2. Date 1.9.15]

Place	Date	Hour	Summary of Events and Information	Remarks and references to Appendices
DROUYIN	3.8.15	—	Billeted from 3rd August till 1st Sept. On Post Duty.	

C J Th——— Lieut.
CAPTN.,
COMMANDING 15th DIV. CYCLIST COMPY.

1577 Wt. W10791/1773 500,000 1/15 D. D. & L. A.D.S.S./Forms/C. 2118.

b/
7050

September 1915.

15th Battn.

15th Bn Ls Cadst Cy:
Pte III
Sept. 15.

deserter some of the surprise
sentry in & around dists &
"Hill 70" Op 25/9/15

JL
23/10/15

Army Form C. 2118.

WAR DIARY
or
INTELLIGENCE SUMMARY.
(Erase heading not required.)

Instructions regarding War Diaries and Intelligence Summaries are contained in F. S. Regs., Part II. and the Staff Manual respectively. Title pages will be prepared in manuscript.

Place	Date	Hour	Summary of Events and Information	Remarks and references to Appendices
VAUDRICOURT	2.9.15		Billeted from 2nd Sept till 24th Sept. Company widely distributed on various duties.— 1 Platoon on Road Control Posts, Party of 45 under Divisional Bombing Officer carrying up stores to front line trenches, 18 attached 15th Div. Signal Coy, laying wires & orderlies. Remainder working on construction of dug outs at MAZINGARBE.	
MAZINGARBE	24.9.15	7.30 P.M	Left VAUDRICOURT with 3 Platoons & occupied dug outs in MAZINGARBE, two Platoons on Control Posts. One under A.P.M. for escorting prisoners.	
	25.9.15	11.45 A.M	FIRST ORDER TO MOVE:— At about 11.45 a.m on 25th Sept, received orders to send two platoons to Loos & for the Commander to report to Advanced Div. H. Qrs, for instructions. I therefore reported in person to Div. H. Qrs. & was ordered to report to G.O.C. 46th INF. BRIGADE and to instruct the O.C. 11th M.M.G. BATTERY to do the same. As exact position of H.Q. 46th INF BRIGADE was not known, I was instructed to go to the CHURCH in LOOS where an orderly would meet me with futher orders. However on reaching the CHURCH the no orderly was to be found & the vicinity was being heavily shelled PROGRESS OF DETACHMENT TO LOOS. On passing through QUALITY STREET was told by an Officer that we were urgently	

WAR DIARY or INTELLIGENCE SUMMARY

Army Form C. 2118.

Place	Date	Hour	Summary of Events and Information	Remarks and references to Appendices
	25/9/15		(Cont'd) required so pushed on as quickly as possible. At the German front line trenches the hand on the LENS Road was so bad that cycles had to be carried. This delayed matters. The 11th M.M.G. Battery were likewise affected. I found O.C. Battery & told him we were both to report to G.O.C. 46th Infty Bde. After reforming my leading Platoon we pushed on, & soon after turning off LENS Road came under rifle fire. I increased the pace & got under cover of a wall in the outskirts of LOOS. Two men were hit, & the rear had to take cover from shell fire. Only a small party arrived in LOOS with me. **ADVANCE THROUGH LOOS.** Shortly after arrival in LOOS No 2 Section 11th M.M.G. Battery under Lieut. McFARLANE came up carrying their guns & some ammunition. I therefore left one of my Officers 2nd Lieut. DUNCAN to reform my detachment, told off all the men with me to help carry guns etc for No 2 Section M.M.G. Batty & advanced through LOOS. Lieut McFARLANE went on to reconnoitre & confirm position by map. Having arrived at the situation I sent them on & the party with 2 guns got established in the front	

WAR DIARY or INTELLIGENCE SUMMARY

Army Form C. 2118.

Place	Date	Hour	Summary of Events and Information	Remarks and references to Appendices
	25.9.15		(CONT^D) line on Hill 70. I went back to bring up the remainder of my detachment & also collected some odd men of N° 2 Section M.M.G. Battⁿ who had a hand cart with ammunition. We went forward through Loos & I halted the party under a bank 100^x in rear of the supporting line & went on to reconnoitre & ascertain the situation.	
			RECONNAISSANCE ON HILL 70.	
			On reaching the firing line about the centre of the Hill, I found that all units of the Division were mixed up. I reported to several Commanding Officers but could not find one of the 46th Inf^y Bde. As our lines on the hill were crowded with men I consulted O.C. 7th Cameron as to advisability of withdrawing my detachment after ascertaining what the situation was on the left. I went along our line to the left, discussing the situation with officers en route & finally reached the LA BASSÉE — LENS road about 400^x South of PUITS 14 Bis. where I found a detachment of about 100 R. Scots Fus. This flank appeared to be rather in the air & was being shelled by our own guns. I sought a message to O.C. 7th Cameron explaining the situation & took it back part of the way myself, then returned to my detachment left a squad under Sgt. Scott to assist N° 2 Section M.M.G Battery, sent an officer patrol under 2nd Lieut Duncan	

WAR DIARY
or
INTELLIGENCE SUMMARY.
(Erase heading not required.)

Army Form C. 2118.

Place	Date	Hour	Summary of Events and Information	Remarks and references to Appendices
LOOS	25.9.15		(Cont'd) by a less exposed route further over to the left to gain touch with the 2nd Brigade, ordered one platoon under 2/Lieut CHUBB to withdraw to a communication trench near LOOS CEMETERY & went back myself to report. Then G.S.O.2 of 15th Division explained what I knew of the situation. He wrote message which was despatched in duplicate by 4 of 2nd Lt: CHUBBS platoon back to Div H.Qrs. Received no further orders but was instructed to remain in LOOS. Distribution of Cyclist Detachment was then as follows:— 2nd Lieut CHUBBS Platoon more or less complete in communication trench near LOOS Cemetery. 2nd Lieut D'uncan's [illegible] two sections out with a patrol to left of 15th Division. One squad of his platoon on #11470 with No. 2 Sec: M.M.G. Battery with No 1- Sec: M.M.G. Battery in trench near LOOS Cemetery. He remained with me as orderlies. I attached myself to H.Q. 44th Bde. and later to 45th Bde. when G.O.C. 46th Bde. took over the line & endeavoured to assist with guides and messengers. At about 9.PM as a number of messengers were constantly being required, I got 2/Lt: CHUBBS platoon established in a cellar in LOOS,	

WAR DIARY
or
INTELLIGENCE SUMMARY.
(Erase heading not required.)

Army Form C. 2118.

Place	Date	Hour	Summary of Events and Information	Remarks and references to Appendices
			(CONT'D) 2nd Lieut DUNCAN reported that he had got in touch with 2nd Inf Bde on our left & had explained how our line was situated. As the officer I/c No 1 Sec M.M.G. Battery had been wounded, I ordered him to take over command of this section. Intercommunication was required by firing line on HILL 70 & 2nd Lieut. CHUBB with his platoon maintained trips throughout the night & early morning of the next day 26th. The situation remained the same until early in the afternoon. My detachment got still further split up owing to a party of 2nd Lt. CHUBB's platoon who got separated, being ordered by a Medical officer to act as stretcher bearers & I desired to withdraw & reform. 2nd Lieut D Munro brought out No 1 Sect. M.M.G Battery from the trenches that was being heavily shelled & succeeded in bring them back under heavy fire. BEHIND THE LINE. I reported to DIVISIONAL H.Q. about 4 P.M. on 26th for further orders & was instructed to reform & collect as many men of the Company as possible and report to G.O.C. 46th Inf. Bde. at LOOS ROAD, keep taking up all stragglers with me. I was ordered by G.O.C. 46th Inf Bde to halt near QUARITY STREET, On the evening of 27th Stragglers over the stragglers which I had collected & about 11.30 P.M. received orders to withdraw	

WAR DIARY
or
INTELLIGENCE SUMMARY.
(Erase heading not required.)

Army Form C. 2118.

Place	Date	Hour	Summary of Events and Information	Remarks and references to Appendices
(Cont^d) To Billets in Mazingarbe.			**RECOMMENDATIONS** I would like to bring to your notice the names of the following Officers and N.C.O — 2nd Lieut. R.N. CHUBB. who made numerous journeys through Loos under heavy Artillery fire taking up ammunition to the firing line on Hill 70. 2nd Lieut. T.M. DUNCAN. who successfully carried out a reconnaissance & got in touch with 2nd Inf. Bde. under fire & later took Command of No. 1 Sect: M.M.G. Battery. No. 1585 Sgt. F. Scott. who greatly assisted No. 2 Sect: M.M.G. Battery on Hill 70. remaining there until both guns were disabled.	

CAPTN.,
COMMANDING 15th DIV. CYCLIST COMPY.

121/7517

October 1915.

15th Division

15th Div L. Cyclist Coy:
Vol 4

Oct 15

WAR DIARY
or
INTELLIGENCE SUMMARY.

Army Form C. 2118.

Place	Date	Hour	Summary of Events and Information	Remarks and references to Appendices
MAZINGARBE	27.9.15	2 PM	No billets being available, reoccupied our dug-outs	
DROUVIN	28.9.15	12 Noon	Marched back to DROUVIN	
LABUSSIERE	29.9.15	4:30 PM	Moved back to LABUSSIERE.	
LABUSSIERE	30.9.15 till 3.10.15		Billeted. Made up certain number of deficiencies. Addressed by Corps and Divisional Commanders.	
LAPUGNOY	3.10.15	11:30 AM	Moved to LABUGNOY & Billeted. Physical training, route marches, etc. Road mending.	
HOUCHIN	15.10.15	10:30 AM	Moved up to Houchin & billeted. Repairing roads & cleaning village. Company Parades, close order drill etc. Furnished four sentry posts.	
"	23.10.15	7:30 AM	Received orders that the Company was placed at disposal of G.O.C. 46th Bde. & to report at H.Q. 46th Inf. Bde. in VERMELLES by 9 am returning each night to billets in HOUCHIN. Reported to Brigade Office 1/2 hour in advance of Company & was given instructions to carry on the work of exacting abandoned arms, equipment, stores from the firing trenches to a point on HULLUCH ~ VERMELLES Road, was informed that VERMELLES was constantly shelled. On arrival of Company, stacked cycles by platoons	

WAR DIARY
or
INTELLIGENCE SUMMARY.
(Erase heading not required.)

Army Form C. 2118.

Place	Date	Hour	Summary of Events and Information	Remarks and references to Appendices
HOUCHIN	24/10/15	8:30am	under cover of wall etc in VERMELLES + advanced by platoons into communication trench, each platoon being given orders as to part of trenches they were to clear & were a dump for the lot. was to be formed. Experienced difficulty in keeping the platoon moving in right directions owing to men getting separated & loosing their way in the trenches. Several parties came under hostile shell fire directed on Communication trench & two men were partially buried but were not injured. 5:30 PM returned to VERMELLES & cycled back to HOUCHIN.	
			bicycled into VERMELLES & carried on with same work. Was given a smaller area of the work in & better control of parties was established, not owing to a better knowledge of the trenches. Returned about 5 PM & on getting out of communication trench near VERMELLES came under heavy hostile artillery fire, six shells falling within striking distance of the Company, which was marching by platoons at intervals, to three rear platoons scattered under orders of Lieut. RICHARDS. by which means casualties were avoided	
HOUCHIN	25/10/15	8:30 am	Cycled to VERMELLES & carried on same work no previous day. Quiet day but very wet trenches in a bad state.	

WAR DIARY
or
INTELLIGENCE SUMMARY.
(Erase heading not required.)

Army Form C. 2118.

Place	Date	Hour	Summary of Events and Information	Remarks and references to Appendices
HOUCHIN.	26.10.15		Rested in billets – made up minor deficiencies. Reserve worked to relieve 7th K.O.S.B. who were holding front line trenches in Sub-section D.3 in G.S.d. (N.W. of QUARRIES)	
	27.10.15		Lieut. RICHARDS and 2nd Lt. NICOL went on ahead to take over line & fire a clone for offices in PHILOSOPHE. Company had dinners & paraded at 11.45 a.m., cycling by platoons to PHILOSOPHE where cycles were stored & then marching to VERMELLES where the trenches were entered. VERMELLES was being shelled as the Company passed through & some platoons experienced gas shells. Relief completed by 4 p.m. No.4, No.1, & No.3 Platoons in the fire trench. No.5 + No.6 Platoons in support and No.2 in Reserve in old front line trench. During the night a certain amount of sniping – German trench. Raining heavily. Casualties – 2 men slightly wounded in hands.	
TRENCHES.	28.10.15		Still wet, quiet day. Casualties 1 man shot in stomach by sniper.	
	29.10.15		Heavy shelling of old German front-line. Three casualties in opening-out. Some difficulty in getting them away to Field Ambulance. Dreides to wire No.2 Platoon out of this trench as a new support trench nearly completed. During the night enemy made an attempt against a sap in the "HAIRPIN" held by 10th SCOTTISH RIFLES on our right. 10th SCOTTISH RIFLES replied with 500 Bombs &	

Army Form C. 2118.

WAR DIARY
or
INTELLIGENCE SUMMARY.
(Erase heading not required.)

Place	Date	Hour	Summary of Events and Information	Remarks and references to Appendices
TRENCHES	—	—	and frustrated the attempt. Casualties – 1 man killed, 3 wounded.	
	30.10.15		Considerable shelling, same as previous day. Enemy snipers not active. Casualties Nil.	
	31.10.15		Nothing unusual. Casualties. Nil.	
	1.11.15	2.P.M.	Relieved by "C" Coy. 13th Royal Scots. Certain amount of hostile shelling of our trenches & Communicating trenches. VERMELLES quiet. Marched back to PHILOSOPHE by Platoons, where tea was ready, Cycled back to HOUCHIN, got into billets & had dinner. Raining hard & all very wet – Casualties – Nil.	
HOUCHIN	2.11.15		Sergt. Scott accidently shot in foot.	

[signature]
CAPTN.
COMMANDING 16th DIV. CYCLIST COMPY

15th Div'l. Gds. Coy.
Vol: 55

121/7656

November 1915.

Nov 15

WAR DIARY
or
INTELLIGENCE SUMMARY.

Army Form C. 2118.

Place	Date	Hour	Summary of Events and Information	Remarks and references to Appendices
HOUCHIN	November 1915 2nd-3rd		Resting and cleaning up.	
"	4th		Took over 4 control posts & five others temporarily on the next day.	
"	6th		Paraded 9 a.m. for work in the trenches, cycled to Foss 3, PHILOSOPHE, where tools were drawn, then marched to trenches, worked at improving communication trench (FRENCH ALLEY). Got back to billets 6 P.M.	
"	8th		Worked on trenches, same routine as on 6th. Improving STANFIELD ROAD.	
"	9th		Deepening new communication trench near LE RUTOIRE. Vicinity heavily shelled about noon. One big shell landed two yards from trench. Had to cease work for ½ hour. Casualties nil. Old gun pit near trench probably drew the fire.	
"	10th		Cleaning up.	
"	11th		Same as 9th. Quiet day.	
"	12th		Very wet, remained in billets.	
"	13th	8 a.m.	Proceeded to Baths at NOEUX-LES-MINES. On return moved into billets at DROUVIN. Normal posts relieved.	
DROUVIN	14th		Trench work – improving LE RUTOIRE ALLEY near VERMELLES. Two shells burst close to 7001 platoon when marching back to PHILOSOPHE.	

Army Form C. 2118.

WAR DIARY
or
INTELLIGENCE SUMMARY.
(Erase heading not required.)

Instructions regarding War Diaries and Intelligence Summaries are contained in F. S. Regs., Part II. and the Staff Manual respectively. Title pages will be prepared in manuscript.

Place	Date	Hour	Summary of Events and Information	Remarks and references to Appendices
DROUVIN	NOVEMBER 1915 15th	3.30 p.m.	Paraded & cycled to PHILOSOPHE for night digging. Work on new trench near LE RUTOIRE. Hostile rifle fire - spent bullets dropping in vicinity, 6 casualties hit. Reached billets 11.30 p.m.	
"	16th		Routine same as previous day, worked on same trench. Very quiet.	
"	17th		Resting & cleaning up	
"	18th		Night work, commenced digging new CHAPEL ALLEY Trench near CHAPEL KEEP.	
"	19th		Same as previous day.	
"	20th		Same as previous day	
"	21st		Church Parade.	
"	22nd		Day work on same trench.	
"	23rd		Baths at NOEUX-LES-MINES.	
"	24th		Cleaning up & inspection parade	
"	25th to 27th		Part of CURLEY CRESCENT Trench was handed over to the Company to improve & continue work thereon until put in a satisfactory state. Commenced deepening & revetting. Frosty weather.	
"	28th		Rushed Church Parade.	
"	29th		Continued work on CURLEY CRESCENT. Thaw set in. Got very wet.	
"	30th		Drying & cleaning up.	

[signature]
CAPTN.
COMMANDING 15th DIV. CYCLIST COMPY.

15th Srnl. Cycl. Corp.
Vol: 6

December 1915.

13/7938

WAR DIARY
or
INTELLIGENCE SUMMARY.
(Erase heading not required.)

Army Form C. 2118.

Instructions regarding War Diaries and Intelligence Summaries are contained in F. S. Regs., Part II. and the Staff Manual respectively. Title pages will be prepared in manuscript.

Place	Date	Hour	Summary of Events and Information	Remarks and references to Appendices
DROUVIN.	DECEMBER 1915 1st & 3rd		Working on CURLEY CRESENT, revetting etc; parading 9.am & returning to billets about 5-30 P.M.	
	4th	1:30 P.M.	Paraded for night work in CURLEY CRESENT, worked on the top & shifted back earth from edge of trench so as to take weight off sides.	
	5th		Rested, Control posts relieved	
	6th		Work in the trenches, 1/2 Company by day on CURLEY CRESENT; Revetting made much easier by weight being moved back from edge. Left cycles in VERMELLES. 1/2 company by night, drew tools from 91st Coy R.E. in PHILOSOPHE, & marched from there to VERMELLE & worked on GORDON ALLEY cleaning out bottom of trench. Lt. RICHARD in charge of party, heavy shelling & work has to be discontinued.	
	7th		Coy. Baths at VERQUIN. Control posts relieved.	
		2:30 P.M.	Paraded for night work on GORDON ALLEY, working on the top, shifting earth from edge of trench, @ running water, all very wet, Enemy quiet but a few stray bullets coming over. Casualties 1 sevenly wounded (H/qrs. Preplaced)	
	8th 9th & 10th	9.a.m	Drying & cleaning up Continued work in CURLEY CRESENT. Rested.	

C. O. Richards
CAPTN.,
COMMANDING 15th DIV. CYCLIST COMPY

WAR DIARY
or
INTELLIGENCE SUMMARY.
(Erase heading not required.)

Army Form C. 2118.

Place	Date	Hour	Summary of Events and Information	Remarks and references to Appendices
DROUVIN	11th		Same as on 9th.	
"	12th		Church Parade; control post relieved.	
"	13th	9.30 a.m.	Party under 2nd Lt GUBB sent to collect tools from CURLEY CRESENT.	
"	"	2.30 p.m.	Company Parade to inspect arms & equipment.	
"	14th	6.30 a.m.	Advance party proceeded to HURIONVILLE. 10 a.m. Party of 9 men proceeded with spare cycles & returned in empty transport.	
"	"	11.30 a.m.	Company billets & cycles inspected.	
"	15th	10 a.m.	Company moved into new billets at HURIONVILLE.	
HURIONVILLE	16th		Cleaning up.	
"	17th		Cleaning up and making up deficiencies.	
"	18th		Inspection Parade.	
"	19th		Church Parade.	
"	20th		Orders to move to MINX. Sent off advance party & transport move then cancelled	
"	21st		Company moved to MINX. Great difficulty in finding billets. Very wet.	
MINY	22nd	8.15 a.m.	Work in 3rd line fire trench. Raining. Returned to billets at 4.0 p.m.	
"	23rd	10.30	Company returned to rest Billets at HURIONVILLE.	

CD Richards CAPTN.,
COMMANDING 15th DIV. CYCLIST COMPY.

WAR DIARY
or
INTELLIGENCE SUMMARY.
(Erase heading not required.)

Army Form C. 2118.

Place	Date	Hour	Summary of Events and Information	Remarks and references to Appendices
HURIONVILLE	Dec 1916 24		Cleaning up and inspection parades	
"	25		Christmas Day! Church parades.	
"	26		Cohick Parade.	
"	27	7 am	Running Parade	
"		9 am	Company drill, Platoon athletics swimming, repairing cycles	
"		2 pm	Lecture to N.C.O's on Map reading; Platoon Sergts Beaver received instruction in First Aid	
"	28		Same as on 27th. Route March by Platoons at 9 am — [illegible] on hopeably do ciphers, rapid	
"	29	7 am	Physical training. 9.15 am Company route march, march the ciphers, rapid	
"			extensions to single fronts, rapid concentration on given front.	
"	30	7 am	Physical training 9.15 am Advance guard Scheme	
"		3 pm	Lecture to N.C.O's on Map Reading	
"	31	7 am	Company Drill 10.30 am Interior economy. 1.45 pm Baths.	

C D Richards
CAPTN.,
COMMANDING 15th DIV. CYCLIST COMPY.

15th Sant: Eclogs
vol: 7

WAR DIARY
or
INTELLIGENCE SUMMARY.
(Erase heading not required.)

Army Form C. 2118.

Place	Date	Hour	Summary of Events and Information	Remarks and references to Appendices
HURIONVILLE.	January 1916 1.1.16	1.45 PM	Baths at ROIMBERT.	
"	2.		Church Parade.	
"	3.	9.15 AM	Demonstration march by platoons, map reading.	
"		2.30 PM	Inspection Parade.	
"	4.	9.30	Company route march without cycles, 2nd Lieut. P. McDONAGH joins company	
"	5.		Divisional route march & tactical exercise.	
"	6.		do.-	
"	7.		do.-	
"	8.	1.45 PM	Baths at ROIMBERT.	
"	9.		Church Parade	
"	10.		Advance Guard Scheme with cavalry.	
"	11.		Dismounted attack with cavalry on HURIONVILLE 2nd Lt. A.K. Brown joins the Company.	
"	12.		Scheme with cavalry. Attack on village held by party of cyclists	
"	13.		Cleaning up and Inspection Parade.	
"	14.		do.-	
"	15.	9.15 AM	Company proceeds to billets in MAZINGARBE.	

C.W. McKenzie CAPTN.
COMMANDING 15th DIV. CYCLIST COMPY.

Army Form C. 2118.

WAR DIARY
or
INTELLIGENCE SUMMARY.
(Erase heading not required.)

Instructions regarding War Diaries and Intelligence Summaries are contained in F. S. Regs., Part II. and the Staff Manual respectively. Title pages will be prepared in manuscript.

Place	Date	Hour	Summary of Events and Information	Remarks and references to Appendices
MAZINGARBE	January 1916 16.	7:30 AM	TRENCH MAINTENENCE PARTY take over communication trenches from 1ST. DIV. CYCLIST COY	
"	17.		Fatigue and Inspection Parades for remainder of company not in the trenches	
"	18.		do.-	do.-
"	19.		do.-	do.-
"	20.		do.-	do.-
"	21.	5.0 PM	TRENCH MAINTENENCE PARTY relieved	
"	22.		Fatigue and Inspection Parades for remainder of company not in the trenches	
"	23.		School Parades	
"	24.		Fatigues and Inspection Parades for remainder of company not in the trenches	
"	25.		do.-	
"	26.		Baths at MAZINGARBE for part of company not in the trenches	
"	27.	5.0 PM	Trench relief carried out under heavy shell fire, no Casualties	
"	28.		Fatigue + Inspection Parades, cleaning billets etc.	
"	29.	11.00 AM	Lectures to Officers + N.C.O.s.	
"	30.		School Parades	
"	31.		Fatigue + Inspection Parades, cleaning up billets etc.	

C D Rhukerr Captn.
COMMANDING 15th DIV. CYCLIST COMPY.

15

15th Lychich[?]
vol: 8

Army Form C. 2118.

WAR DIARY
or
INTELLIGENCE SUMMARY.
(Erase heading not required.)

Instructions regarding War Diaries and Intelligence Summaries are contained in F. S. Regs., Part II. and the Staff Manual respectively. Title pages will be prepared in manuscript.

Place	Date	Hour	Summary of Events and Information	Remarks and references to Appendices
MAZINGARBE	FEBRUARY 1916 1.	11.0 am	Lecture to Officers & N.C.O.s on Map reading. Casualties; 1.O.R. wounded in trenches (rifle fire).	
"	2.	2.30 PM	Inspection Parade for remainder of Company not in Trenches.	
"	3.	11.0 am	Lecture to Officers & M.M.s Trench Maintenance Party relieved. Casualties 1.O.R. wounded in trenches (rifle fire)	
"			Remainder of company not in trenches cleaning up uniform & equipment; Casualties, 2.O.R. killed in trenches (shell fire)	
"	4.	11.0 am	Lecture to Officers & N.C.O.s not in the Trenches.	
"	5.	11.0 am	Lecture to Officers & N.C.O.s. Shell burst in billet. Casualties; 2.O.R. wounded.	
"	6.		Church parade. Shell burst into billet. Casualties, 1.O.R. wounded	
"	7.		Remainder of Company not in Trenches, move to billets in Drouvin. Capt H. Burke appointed Bde Major 46th Infantry Brigade	
DROUVIN	8.		Trench Maintenance Party relieved	
"	9.		Remainder of Company not in Trenches, cleaning billets, cycles and equipment.	
"	10.	9.30 am	Inspection Parades for remainder of company not in Trenches	
"	11.	9.30 am	Dismounted drill and handling of arms	
"	12.	"	Inspection of Smoke Helmets & practice in use of same	
"	13.	"	Church Parade for remainder of company not in Trenches.	
"	14.	10.0 am	Baths at NOEUX-LES-MINES for remainder of company not in trenches.	
"		4.30 PM	Trench Maintenance Party Relieved	

1577 Wt. W10791/1773 500,000 1/15 D. D. & L. A.D.S.S./Forms/C. 2118.

Army Form C. 2118.

WAR DIARY
or
INTELLIGENCE SUMMARY.
(Erase heading not required.)

Instructions regarding War Diaries and Intelligence Summaries are contained in F. S. Regs., Part II. and the Staff Manual respectively. Title pages will be prepared in manuscript.

Place	Date	Hour	Summary of Events and Information	Remarks and references to Appendices
DROUVIN	15		Day spent by men relieved from trenches in cleaning uniform, equipment, etc.	
"	16	8.45am	Inspection Parade for remainder of company not in trenches.	
"	17	11.0 am	Kit inspection and issue of stores to complete mens kits & equipment.	
"	18	9.45am	Lecture to N.C.O.s on Trench Maintenance	
"	19		Insp. of cycles and inspection of same, for remainder of company not in trenches.	
"	20		Trench Maintenance Party relieved.	
"	21		Day spent by men relieved from trenches in cleaning equipment, cycles, etc	
"	22	10.am	Inspection Parades for remainder of company not in trenches	
"	23	8.45am	Baths at NOEUX-LES-MINES	
"	24	10.0am	Route march without cycles for remainder of company not in trench.	
"		3.0 PM	Lecture to N.C.O.s	
"	25	10.am	Inspection of boots, smoke helmets etc, for remainder of company not in trenches.	
"		2.30 PM	Insp. of cycles and inspection of same,	
"	26		Trench Maintenance Party, relieved.	
"	27		Church parade for men relieved from trenches	
"	28	10.0AM	Inspection of Smoke helmets, rifles, etc	

Army Form C. 2118.

WAR DIARY
or
INTELLIGENCE SUMMARY.
(Erase heading not required.)

Instructions regarding War Diaries and Intelligence Summaries are contained in F. S. Regs., Part II. and the Staff Manual respectively. Title pages will be prepared in manuscript.

Place	Date	Hour	Summary of Events and Information	Remarks and references to Appendices
DROUVIN.	28.	2.30pm	Section order drill & handling of arms for men not in trenches.	
"	29.		For remainder of Company not in trenches, baths at NOEUX-LES-MINES.	

C M Michard — CAPTN.
COMMANDING 15th DIV. CYCLIST COMPY.

15 D 3
Eye Coy
Vol 9

WAR DIARY
or
INTELLIGENCE SUMMARY

Army Form C. 2118.

(Erase heading not required.)

Instructions regarding War Diaries and Intelligence Summaries are contained in F. S. Regs., Part II. and the Staff Manual respectively. Title pages will be prepared in manuscript.

Place	Date	Hour	Summary of Events and Information	Remarks and references to Appendices
DROUVIN	1-3-16		Inspection of Smoke Helmets, equipment etc.	
"	2-3-16		Dismounted Route March and Map reading for remainder of company not in trenches	
"	3-3-16	3-30pm	Trench Maintenance Party relieved.	
"	4-3-16		Joint fly relieved party in cleaning cycles, equipment, clothing etc.	
"	5-3-16		Church Parade	
"	6-3-16		Baths at NOEUX-LES-MINES for remainder of company not in trenches	
"	7-3-16		Close order drill and handling of arms	
"	8-3-16		Map reading, Lecture to officers and N.C.O.s	
"	9-3-16	3/30pm	Trench Maintenance Party relieved.	
"	10-3-16		Joint fly relieved party in cleaning cycles, equipment, etc.	
"	11-3-16		Company move to billets in VAUDRICOURT	
VAUDRICOURT	12-3-16		Church Parade	
"	13-3-16	8-15am	Baths at NOEUX-LES-MINES for remainder of company not in trenches	
"	"	5-0pm	Night Disposn on (BOLK IT ALLEY). Returned to billets at 2-30 am 14-3-16	
"	14-3-16		Joint in cleaning up & inspection parades.	
"	15-3-16	3/30am	Trench Maintenance Party relieved.	

Army Form C. 2118.

WAR DIARY
or
INTELLIGENCE SUMMARY.
(Erase heading not required.)

Instructions regarding War Diaries and Intelligence Summaries are contained in F. S. Regs., Part II. and the Staff Manual respectively. Title pages will be prepared in manuscript.

Place	Date	Hour	Summary of Events and Information	Remarks and references to Appendices
VAUDRICOURT.	16.3.16		Spent by party just relieved from trenches in cleaning equipment, cycles, etc.	
"	17.3.16	9.30am	Company inspection for men not in trenches.	
"	18.3.16	9.0am	Cleaning of cycles. 1 Sergt. & 12 men on manoeuvres with cavalry	
"	19.3.16		Church Parade.	
"	20.3.16	7.15am	Baths at NOEUX-LES-MINES for men not in trenches. Company parade at 2.30pm	
"	21.3.16	3.30	Trench Maintenance Party relieved. Lecture to N.C.O.s at 4.30.	
"	22.3.16		Morning spent by men just relieved from trenches in cleaning equipment etc. Inspection in afternoon of same	
"	23.3.16	8.0am	Remainder of company not in trenches on Manoeuvres with cavalry. Inspection by G.O.C. 15th Division	
"	24.3.16	9.30am	Company parade for men not in trenches	
"	25.3.16	8.30am	Control posts taken over. Inspection of cycles for remainder of company.	
"	26.3.16	6.30am	Party of 1 Sergt. & 9 men working with R.E.s at MINY.	
"		10.30am	Party of 1 Sergt. & 12 men on duty on control posts. Trench Maintenance Party relieved by 16th Div. Cyclists	
"	27.3.16	9.15am	Company move to new billets at AURIONVILLE.	
AURIONVILLE.	28.3.16		Morning devoted to cleaning + tidying cycles. Afternoon in cleaning riding equipment.	
"	29.3.16	2.15pm	Company inspection at PHILOMEL by G.O.C. 15th Division.	
"	30.3.16	7.40am	Bath at RAIMBERT. Inspection for condemning unserviceable clothing	
"	31.3.16		Preparing for move to SAMER to join 3rd Cavalry Division	

1577 Wt. W10791/1773 500,000 1/15 D. D. & L. A.D.S.S./Forms/C. 2118.

[Signature]
CAPTN.,
COMMANDING 15th DIV. CYCLIST COMPY.

Army Form C. 2118.

15 Dn Cycles
Vol 10

WAR DIARY
or
INTELLIGENCE SUMMARY.
(Erase heading not required.)

Instructions regarding War Diaries and Intelligence Summaries are contained in F. S. Regs., Part II. and the Staff Manual respectively. Title pages will be prepared in manuscript.

Place	Date	Hour	Summary of Events and Information	Remarks and references to Appendices
Hurionville	1/4/16	7.30 am	Company paraded for march to SAMER, for continued cavalry manoeuvres.	
Thirouanne	2/4/16	7.30 "	Company continued march to Samer. Thines to Bondette.	
Bondette	3/4/16	7. am	Morning devoted to cleaning cycles & Equipment. Inspection by O.C. Company at 2 P.M.	
"	4/4/16	8.15 "	Coy Drill in at 8.15 a.m. fit a route march. No C.O.'s parade at 2.30 P.M. for lecture.	
"	5/4/16	8.0 am	Coy paraded at 8. a.m. for manoeuvres with 1st Cav. Division	
"	6/4/16	8.0 am	fully 1 Coy on manoeuvres with 1st Cav. Div. Other half on Route March. Lecture to hCO's 5 P.M.	
"	7/4/16	8. am	Coy on manoeuvres with 1st Cav. Div. Lecture to Officers & NCO's at 5 P.M.	
"	8/4/16	8. am	Coy on manoeuvres with 1st Cav. Div. Lecture to Officers & NCO's at 5 P.M.	
"	9/4/16	9 am	Coy spent the morning in cleaning up. C.O. attended Divine Service in Samer at 5 P.M.	
"	10/4/16	8. am	Coy on manoeuvres with 1st Cav. Div. Lecture to Officers & NCO's at 5 P.M.	
"	11/4/16	8. am	Coy spent the morning cleaning & overhauling cycles. Baths for boy at 3 P.M.	
"	12/4/16	8. am	Coy went out on night manoeuvres. Falling in at 1.a.m. Having Breakfast on return.	
"	13/4/16	9 am	Coy on manoeuvres with 1st Cav. Div. Lecture to Officers & N.C.O's at 5 P.M.	
"	14/4/16	8. am	Coy on manoeuvres with 1st Cav. Div. Lecture to Officers & N.C.O's at 5 P.M.	
"	15/4/16	8.30 "	Coy spent the morning cleaning cycles. Inspection by O.C. 2.30 P.M.	
"	16/4/16	10.30	Morning spent cleaning billets. Divine Service – R&'s 10 am	

Army Form C. 2118.

WAR DIARY
or
INTELLIGENCE SUMMARY.
(Erase heading not required.)

Instructions regarding War Diaries and Intelligence Summaries are contained in F. S. Regs., Part II. and the Staff Manual respectively. Title pages will be prepared in manuscript.

Place	Date	Hour	Summary of Events and Information	Remarks and references to Appendices
Lozinghem	17/4/16	7.30 a.m.	Coy fell in at 7.30 A.M. for return journey to Hurionville	
Lozingues	18/4/16	9 a.m.	Coy again resumed move to Hurionville	
Hurionville	19/4/16	8.30 "	Morning spent in cleaning bycles & Equipment. Inspection by C.O. Coy at 2.30 P.M.	
"	20/4/16	11.30 "	Inspection of Coy Cycles at 11.30 A.M. Coy bow drill in the afternoon.	
"	21/4/16	8.30	2 Platoons on Rifle Range. The remaining four out on route march.	
"	22/4/16	7.30	Coy out for Baths at Raimbert. Cleaning of Cycles at 11.30 P.M. Inspection of Same at 2.30 P.M.	
"	23/4/16		Church Parade.	
"	24/4/16	6.45 a.m.	Standing in Seaforts + Others forces to moving Parade at 9 a.m. for foot march. Parade at 2 P.M. for Coy Drill.	
"	25/4/16	7 a.m.	Cleaning up Cycles & Equipment. Inspection of Same at 11 a.m. Inspection of Personnel at 2.30 P.M.	
"	26/4/16	9 a.m.	Parade for move to Donquineul.	
Donquineul	27/4/16	9 a.m.	Parade for Close bow drill by Platoons. Parade 2.30 P.M. for Maps Reading.	
"	28/4/16	9 "	Parade for Close bow drill by Platoons 9 P.M. Parade at 2.30 for Cycle Drill.	
"	29/4/16	9 "	Coy Parade for inspection 9.30 A.M. Parade in the afternoon for Inoculation.	

Ed. P.R. Grant CAPTN.,
COMMANDING 15th DIV. CYCLIST COMPY.

To
A.G's. Office
Base.

[STAMP: 15TH DIVISIONAL CYCLIST COMPANY ORDERLY ROOM No. C.1 Date 29-5-16.]

Herewith War Diary of the 15th Divisional Cyclist Company for month ending 29-5-16.

In the Field
29-5-16.

A.R.Brown 2/L
for CAPTN.,
COMMANDING 15th DIV. CYCLIST COMPY.

WAR DIARY or INTELLIGENCE SUMMARY

Army Form C. 2118.

Vol. 11

16th DIVISIONAL CYCLIST COMPANY — ORDERLY ROOM
No. 10. Date 29.5.16

Place	Date	Hour	Summary of Events and Information	Remarks and references to Appendices
Jonqueuil	1/5/16	—	Coy resting after inoculation on previous day.	
"	2/5/16	10 A.M.	Coy parade for medical inspection by Capt. Taylor. R.A.M.C.	
"	3/5/16	7.40 A.M.	Coy out as working party — digging trenches at Gonnay.	
"	4/5/16	"	Coy out as working party — digging trenches at Gonnay.	
"	5/5/16	"	Coy out as working party — digging trenches at Gonnay.	
"	6/5/16	"	Coy out as working party — digging trenches at Gonnay.	
"	7/5/16	10. A.M.	Inspection of Company and Cycles by O.C. Company. Service for 61/6 at 12.30 P.M.	
"	8/5/16	8.30 A.M.	Company on manoeuvres with Divisional Cavalry.	
"	9/5/16	7.40 A.M.	Company out as working party — digging trenches at Gonnay.	
"	10/5/16	7.40 A.M.	Company out as working party — digging trenches at Gonnay.	
"	11/5/16	7.40 A.M.	Company out as working party — digging trenches at Gonnay.	
"	12/5/16	—	Company standing to arms.	
"	13/5/16	—	Company standing to arms.	
"	14/5/16	—	Company standing to arms.	
"	15/5/16	—	Company standing to arms.	
"	16/5/16	—	Company standing to arms.	

Army Form C. 2118.

WAR DIARY
or
INTELLIGENCE SUMMARY.
(Erase heading not required.)

Instructions regarding War Diaries and Intelligence Summaries are contained in F. S. Regs., Part II. and the Staff Manual respectively. Title pages will be prepared in manuscript.

Place	Date	Hour	Summary of Events and Information	Remarks and references to Appendices
Longuenesse	17/5/16	—	Company Standing to Arms	
"	18/5/16	8 am	Company cleaning bytes. 2.30 P.M. Inspection of same by platoons	
"	19/5/16	6.45 P.M.	Company employed as working party in the Trenches with Signal Coy.	
"	20/5/16	6.45 P.M.	Company employed as working party in the Trenches with Signal Coy.	
"	21/5/16	6.45 P.M.	Company employed as working party in the Trenches with Signal Coy.	
"	22/5/16	6.45 P.M.	Company employed as working party in the Trenches with Signal Coy.	
"	23/5/16	6.45 P.M.	Company employed as working party in the Trenches with Signal Coy.	
"	24/5/16	6.45 P.M.	Company employed as working party in the Trenches with Signal Coy.	
"	25/5/16	6.45 P.M.	Company employed as working party in the Trenches with Signal Coy.	
"	26/5/16	6.45 P.M.	Company employed as working party in the Trenches with Signal Coy.	
"	27/5/16	2.30 P.M.	Cleaning Equipment and mending + cleaning Clothing	
"	28/5/16	8.30 am.	Baths at BETHUNE. 2.30 P.M. Inspection of Clothing & Equipment.	
"	29/5/16	12.30 a.m.	Orders to proceed direct to Divisional Headquarters. Finding an attack by the Enemy	

A.N. Brown Lt CAPTN.,
COMMANDING 15th DIV. CYCLIST COMPY.

www.ingramcontent.com/pod-product-compliance
Lightning Source LLC
Chambersburg PA
CBHW081458160426
43193CB00013B/2521